Angry at God?

Bring Him Your Doubts and Questions

Resources for Changing Lives

A Ministry of
THE CHRISTIAN COUNSELING AND EDUCATIONAL FOUNDATION
Glenside, Pennsylvania

RCL Ministry Booklets
Susan Lutz, Series Editor

Angry at God?

Bring Him Your Doubts and Questions

Robert D. Jones

P&R
P U B L I S H I N G
P.O. BOX 817 • PHILLIPSBURG • NEW JERSEY 08865-0817

Printed in the United States of America

Library of Congress Cataloging-in-Publication Data

Jones, Robert D., 1959-
Angry at God? : bring Him your doubts and questions / Robert D. Jones.
p. cm. — (Resources for changing lives)
Includes bibliographical references.
ISBN 0-87552-691-8
1. Anger—Religious aspects—Christianity. 2. Suffering—Religious aspects—Christianity. 3. Providence and government of God. 4. Spiritual life—Christianity. 5. Consolation. I. Title. II. Series.
BV4627.A5 J66 2003
231'.8—dc21

2002033387

Carolyn was confused. Ray's affair stunned her. Matters worsened when he refused to break off the relationship. The final blow—his decision to stay with the other woman—simply shattered Carolyn's life.

Questions about Ray, the other woman, and what Carolyn should do flooded her thoughts. *What was he thinking? How could he throw away our fourteen years? Why her? How will I provide for myself? Will the divorce get ugly?*

As the initial shock gradually subsided, another, tougher crop of questions slowly emerged. *Where was God in all of this? How could a good Christian like Ray turn away from what he knew to be right? Why would the Lord let the kids and me face such a nightmare? Is this what a good God does to his people?*

Carolyn was becoming angry at God, and she knew it.

What should she do about it? Was it okay to be angry with God? Several Christian friends urged her to "do the right thing" and not question God. But for Carolyn, this seemed too stoical. She felt angry! Was she supposed to simply paste on a good, Christian, plastic smile? Was she to ignore her overwhelming doubts about God's dealings? Was the radio preacher right when he said that "good Christians don't complain" in the face of trials?

Other friends recommended a different path. They encouraged her to vent her feelings to God. "It's okay to be angry with God. In fact, given what you're going through, it's healthy. Don't stuff it. Tell him how you feel. Be honest; he already knows. Tell him you're angry. He'll understand. He's a big boy. He can handle it."

Carolyn was confused. The thought of expressing her anger *to* God made sense. It seemed so refreshing and freeing. Yet she was harboring some deep doubts about God's trustworthiness, and her conscience wasn't clear about venting so freely. To her, it felt like blasphemy.

Your Situation

Your circumstances, of course, may differ from Carolyn's. Maybe your boss fired you unfairly. Or an adult abused you as a child. Or someone you trusted betrayed you. Maybe you face financial burdens with no relief in sight, or a progressive, debilitating disease. Or maybe it's less definable. You are plodding through life with constant disappointment, a kind of pervasive inner sadness. You lack the joy that marks many Christians you know.

Whatever your specific situation, what you share with Carolyn are nagging questions about God. You mistrust his goodness. You question his wisdom. You tense up when you think of him being "in control" of your life in all its misery. In short, you too are angry at God.

What should you do? The good news from God's Word is that we are not left with only two options. We are not forced to choose between hiding our soul's struggles from God and venting our anger at him. The Bible rejects both in favor of a third way, a middle path that encourages transparency without endorsing blasphemy.

Let's state this in two principles, examining each in turn.

It Is Wrong to Be Angry at God

Is it okay to hold in your heart, or voice with your mouth, anger against God? No. The

Bible forbids the vent-your-feelings-against-God approach.

Anger in the Bible is a whole-person judgment we make against a perceived wrong. We react negatively in our mind, emotions, and will against what we conclude to be evil or unfair. In this sense, anger is not merely a morally neutral emotion ("It's neither right nor wrong, it just is," as some naively argue) that exists apart from one's inner beliefs, affections, emotions, and volitions. Instead, anger is a function of our judgment. We perceive something or someone to be wrong, and we respond accordingly with our whole being.

Framed this way, the answer to our "Is it okay to be angry with God?" question is clear: No! Anger against God is wrong because it accuses God of wrongdoing. To be angry with God is to perceive some wrong in God, to apprehend some evil in his ways.

What is the root issue? Kay Arthur insightfully cuts to the core. You get angry at God, she observes, "because God did not do what you thought he should or the way he should do it or when he should do it."[1] Notice that we accuse God of not doing *what* (actions or inaction) he should do, or not doing it in *the way* (manner) he should, or *when* (timing) he should. In short, we want what we want when we want it, and when God does not deliver, we judge him.

Biblical Examples

The Bible offers numerous examples of people who were angry at God. Genesis 4 records God's rejection of Cain and his offering and his acceptance of Abel and his offering.

> The LORD looked with favor on Abel and his offering, but on Cain and his offering he did not look with favor. So Cain was very angry, and his face was downcast. Then the LORD said to Cain, "Why are you angry? Why is your face downcast? If you do what is right, will you not be accepted? But if you do not do what is right, sin is crouching at your door; it desires to have you, but you must master it." (Gen. 4:4b–7)

Cain wanted God to accept his sacrifice on his terms; he believed God *should* do so. When God in his holiness refused Cain's demand, Cain reacted in anger against God (along with depression, jealousy, and the murder of his brother). Cain may not have voiced this anger, but God saw it.

Was Cain's anger justified? The answer is obvious. Cain's anger at God was sinful. His sinful motives and beliefs drove his anger. He needed to repent of the sin that sought to master him and instead do what was right.

In 1 Chronicles 13, tragedy interrupted David's plan to return God's ark to Jerusalem. While the Israelites were transporting it, a leader named Uzzah "reached out his hand to steady the ark, because the oxen stumbled" (v. 9). This seemingly innocent act violated God's explicit command in Numbers 4:15 not to touch the ark. Uzzah disregarded God's holiness and God responded with wrath. "The LORD's anger burned against Uzzah, and he struck him down because he had put his hand on the ark. So he died there before God" (1 Chron. 13:10).

How did King David respond to God's action? "Then David was angry because the LORD's wrath had broken out against Uzzah. . . . David was afraid of God that day. . . ." (vv. 11–12). Most commentators agree that David believed that God's wrath was too harsh. David judged God to be wrong in his actions, at least in their seeming severity. Having placed God on trial, David declared God guilty.

One wonders if David had fallen prey to the "After all I've done for you, this is the thanks I get?" mentality that arises within us when God allows hardships into our lives. We believe that God owes us something better than the providential hardships we face. For Carolyn, it involved subtle demands that God treat her nicely because she had been a faithful wife, loving mother, and good Christian for fourteen years.

The operative clause in all such lies is this: God *should* have. We can imagine David's mutterings: "Surely, God, you should have overlooked Uzzah's well-intentioned mistake." Or, "You should have punished him later, or in private, or less drastically. Your swift and harsh stroke undermined the morale of our mission—the mission we were doing for you, I might add!"

Though the narrative cites no explicit condemnation, the context implies divine disapproval of David's anger, especially in light of David's fearful decision to abort the mission. One can hardly conclude from this text that it is okay to be angry at God.

Or consider Jonah. God called his prophet to preach salvation to pagan Nineveh, Israel's enemy. Jonah reluctantly complied. Nineveh repented, God withdrew his wrath, and Jonah became angry with God.

> When God saw what they did and how they turned from their evil ways, he had compassion and did not bring upon them the destruction he had threatened.
>
> But Jonah was greatly displeased and became angry. He prayed to the LORD, "O LORD, is this not what I said when I was still at home? That is why I was so quick to flee to Tarshish. I knew that you are a gracious and compassionate God, slow to anger and abounding in love, a God who relents from sending calamity. Now, O LORD, take away my life, for it is better for me to die than to live."
>
> But the LORD replied, "Have you any right to be angry?"
>
> Jonah went out and sat down at a place east of the city. There he made himself a shelter, sat in its shade and waited to see what would happen to the city. Then the LORD God provided a vine and made it grow up over Jonah to give shade for his head to ease his dis-

comfort, and Jonah was very happy about the vine. But at dawn the next day God provided a worm, which chewed the vine so that it withered. When the sun rose, God provided a scorching east wind, and the sun blazed on Jonah's head so that he grew faint. He wanted to die, and said, "It would be better for me to die than to live."

But God said to Jonah, "Do you have a right to be angry about the vine?"

"I do," he said. "I am angry enough to die."

But the LORD said, "You have been concerned about this vine, though you did not tend it or make it grow. It sprang up overnight and died overnight. But Nineveh has more than a hundred and twenty thousand people who cannot tell their right hand from their left, and many cattle as well. Should I not be concerned about that great city?" (Jonah 3:10–4:10)

What produced Jonah's anger? His evil heart. He craved his enemies' destruction more than the glory God would gain through their conversion. Jonah did not love his neighbor as himself. Neither love for his enemies nor compassion for the needy ruled him. Jonah believed that God had not acted the way the God of Israel should have acted.

What was God's attitude toward Jonah's anger? God disapproved. He undercut Jonah's supposed "right" to be angry. Jonah's outburst was the venting of his sinful flesh, and God exposed it as such. It was not okay for Jonah—or anyone—to be angry at God.

We could cite other biblical examples of anger against God: the rebel kings of Psalm 2, Job's wife in Job 2, King Asa in 2 Chronicles 16 (against God's prophet), and the Jewish crowd against Jesus in John 7:23. Each reveals the same themes. Anger against God is always wrong in that it accuses God of evil.

Accusations Against God

John Calvin's pastoral insights into this matter remain unsurpassed. In his sermon from Job 1:22 ("Through all this Job did not sin nor did he blame God," NASB), Calvin asks:

> Why is it that men fret so when God sends them things entirely contrary to their desire, except that they do not ac-

> knowledge that God does everything by reason and that he has just cause? For if we had well-imprinted on our *hearts* "All that God does is founded in good reason" it is certain that we would be ashamed to chafe so against him when, I say, we know that he has *just* occasion to dispose thus of things, as we see. Now, therefore, it is especially said that Job attributed to God nothing without reason, that is to say, that *he did not imagine that God did anything which was not just and equitable*[2] (emphasis added).

Here lies the root problem beneath our anger against God. We accuse him of injustice. Calvin continues:

> As soon as God does not send what *we have desired*, we dispute against him, we bring suit, not that we appear to do this, but our manner shows that this is nevertheless our intent. We consider every blow, "And why has thus happened?" But from what spirit is this pronounced? From a *poisoned heart*, as if we said, "The thing *should have been other-*

> *wise, I see no reason for this.*" Meanwhile God will be *condemned* among us. This is how men exasperate themselves. And in this what do they do? It is as if they *accused* God of being a tyrant or a hair-brain who asked only to put everything in confusion. Such horrible *blasphemy* blows out of the mouths of men[3] (emphasis added).

Is it okay to be angry at God? No. It is to call God a "hair-brain" and to voice "horrible blasphemy." How should we counter this tendency? Calvin concludes:

> However, the Holy Spirit wished to tell us that, if we wish to render glory to God and to bless his name properly, *we must be persuaded that God does nothing without reason.* So then, let us not attribute to him either cruelty or ignorance, as if he did things in spite and unadvisedly, but let us acknowledge that he proceeds in everything with admirable justice, with goodness and infinite wisdom, so that *there is only entire uprightness or equity in all that he does*[4] (emphasis added).

The solution to sinful anger at God lies in continually repenting of our remaining unbelief and rebellion. We must reject the lies that deny God's goodness, power, and wisdom, and we must reaffirm his righteousness, love, and justice. We must repent, knowing that "God opposes the proud, but gives grace to the humble" (James 4:6).

While Carolyn never read Calvin and might have winced at the thought of calling God a "hair brain," these same truths needed to penetrate her heart. As she studied the Scripture passages listed above, she began to see that the root of her anger with God was her subtle accusations against him: *God should not let this nightmare happen to me and to good Christian families like mine.*

God's Sovereign Purposes

Before turning to our second principle—the one that guided Carolyn toward God in a positive direction—let's consider a common variation of the first principle. As a mature Christian, Carolyn knew up front that God was involved in her trial situation; this was what prompted her questions about his actions.

Don, however, did not blame God for any

of his problems, at least not initially. Don was quick to blame his misery on his job—a demanding boss, unscrupulous competitors, and disloyal clients—and on his lower back injury, and the physical and financial problems it brought. He was chronically angry at others and "just upset at life overall."

In one sense Don was committed to the Lord. He was regularly involved in worship and sought to pray and read Scripture several times a week. That is why he protested his pastor's suggestion that he was angry at God without realizing it.

Like many Christians, Don failed to see God's sovereign hand behind his life's hardships. Yet, as Don came to realize, his problems were not random occurrences of blind chance. They came to him as the providential dealings of the omnipotent Ruler who "does whatever pleases him" (Ps. 115:3). Don had not seen that God is the ultimate cause of every hardship and that he uses every trial for the good purpose of making us like Jesus Christ (Gen. 50:20; Job 1–2; 38–42; Rom. 8:28–29).

The first turning point for Don came when he saw that God, in his sovereignty, had placed Don precisely where he wanted him to be. Yet this produced a whole new problem for Don.

Before, he had been angry at "life," at "other people," at "nature," and "the world" in general. As long as the Lord was marginal in Don's mind, Don had never blamed him for his hardships. But when God became central—when Don granted God his rightful place in the middle of his life struggles—he became angry at God. He began hauling the Lord into court.

Was this progress for Don? Actually, yes! This was the first and necessary step in a process toward deeper, more lasting joy. To move from ignorance to an awareness of God's sovereignty signals progress. The next step came as he studied God's good purposes in sending such trials. Like Carolyn and countless other saints, Don saw that the sovereign God who stood behind his thorn-infested job and injured back was also his loving Father. He gradually saw from Scripture that the Lord was using these trials to make him more like Jesus, to draw him closer to himself, to expose his own remaining sin, to taste something of what his Savior suffered, to equip him for compassionate ministry toward others, and even to increase his longing for Christ's return and the new body and new earth Christ promised him. As Don reflected on these and similar truths, his anger at God gave way to trust in God. Don was learning to repent of his demands that God act a certain way. He was learning to love God for using these hardships for gracious purposes.

It Is Right to Express Your Questions to God with a Heart of Faith

If anger against God is sin, how do we deal with our doubts and questions about his providential dealings, especially amid our sufferings? Must we stoically, silently "stuff" our struggles? Thankfully, our Lord presents another option, the path laid out for us through the lament portions of Scripture.

Christians are sometimes baffled by God's ways and confused by his apparent inconsistencies. Yet Scripture teaches us the art of holy lamenting—learning how to complain in faith—to God about the calamities he sends.

For example, the careful reader of Job 1 and 2 cannot avoid the conclusion that God himself is the ultimate cause of Job's misfortune. In the chapters that follow we hear Job's bitter complaints and heart-wrenching questions. Yet he never crossed over into a settled state of blaming God for his suffering. While Job's questions were never answered, he remained at heart faithful to God. The Lord he came to know in bolder, overwhelming ways in Job 42 was the same Lord he had trusted from the beginning.

We see the same thing in Jeremiah's book of Lamentations. He winces when he recalls God's hand of judgment on his own nation. He attributes the devastation to God's decrees, yet he never denies God's covenant loyalty or essential goodness to his people. He does not impugn God's motives or accuse him of malice or capriciousness. He wrestles, he wonders, and he questions, but he ultimately rests in God's promises of restoration and blessing.

Consider also the prophet, Habakkuk, on the eve of the Babylonian invasion (c. 600 B.C.). His honest complaints (Hab. 1:1–3, 12–2:1) arise not from anger against God but from the conviction that God was indeed a powerful Judge and a loving Savior (3:18–19). His questions reflect his fundamental faith.

Of course, the richest deposit of biblical lament lies in the Psalms. Listen to David's cries in Psalm 13:

> How long, O LORD? Will you forget
> me forever?
> How long will you hide your face
> from me?

How long must I wrestle with my thoughts
and every day have sorrow in my heart?
How long will my enemy triumph over me?

Look on me and answer, O LORD my God.
Give light to my eyes, or I will sleep in death;
my enemy will say, "I have overcome him,"
and my foes will rejoice when I fall.

But I trust in your unfailing love;
my heart rejoices in your salvation.
I will sing to the LORD,
for he has been good to me.

David grapples with God's apparent distance from him in the midst of enemy attacks. He questions the Lord's seeming neglect and complains about God's felt absence. Yet notice that David speaks *to* his God. He has dealings *with* God. He addresses God *directly*. And instead of accusing God of wrongdoing, David's fourfold "how long" lamentation (vv. 1–2) leads to petition (vv. 3–4), which yields confession of trust (v. 5) and commitment to praise (v. 6). He resolves to trust in God's loyal love, salvation, and goodness.

Laments of Faith

What common elements can we glean from these biblical laments?

1. Suffering. Each of these believers was experiencing intense confusion and bewilderment over apparent inconsistencies between God's revealed character and his current, providential dealings. Carolyn's divorce was no less tragic than the sufferings these believers faced. Don's work and back problems were comparable to the trials recorded in Scripture. The Bible puts words to our suffering by recording the words of other sufferers.

2. Prayer. Each lamenter voiced his questions directly to God himself. They moved *toward* God, not *away* from him. They sought his face in prayer and settled for nothing less than conversational contact with their Savior. Job, Jeremiah, David, and Habakkuk all had direct dealings *with* God. One of Carolyn's problems was that she was asking questions *about* God but not bringing those questions *to* him.

3. Faith. Their laments arose from fundamental faith (albeit imperfect). In the trenches

they submitted to God and clung to basic truths about his person and work. In fact, it was their belief in God's absolute sovereignty, power, wisdom, and goodness that produced their complaints in the first place! The mindset goes like this: Father, it is precisely *because* I know that you are all-loving and all-powerful that I am struggling with the seeming absence of your love and power right now in this situation. It is *because* I am convinced that you are good that your chastisements confuse me. It is *because* I believe in your covenant love that your apparent distance baffles me.

4. Humility. These believers expressed their laments with reverence and submission. They didn't vent or lose control. By humbling themselves, they avoided the blasphemous accusations found in pagan religious literature.

5. Renewal. These saints reached some resolution of their struggle, a measure of renewal in their faith. The closing sections of Job, Lamentations, Habakkuk, and Psalm 13 all echo a mature faith, tried and tested, riper and sweeter through the hardship.

God's Agenda in Suffering

Alex, a committed Christian worker, faced problems of depression and withdrawal that were tied to nightmares and memories of a childhood rape by several older boys. His struggles seriously affected his marriage and ministry. After three months of therapy that was not biblically driven and which yielded few results, he sought the help of a Christ-centered, biblical counselor.

At the root level, Alex doubted God's goodness because of this abuse. The "anger at God" question nagged him. The previous counselor had given him a book that pushed an "It's okay to be angry with God" agenda. The author urged Alex to let out his anger, and even to forgive God. Fortunately, Alex didn't buy into this approach; his biblical instincts raised red flags.

What was wrong? Like many of us, Alex had mistakenly interpreted God's heart based on his interpretation of God's providence. As his new counselor helped him look at his life through a biblical lens, Alex gained a more accurate view of his heavenly Father.

Viewing the rape incident under the biblical category of trials opened a new vista of insight and hope for Alex. He saw some of God's purposes for this trial through studying James 1:1–12, 2 Corinthians 1, Job, and the life of Joseph in Genesis 37–50.

Using Psalm 77—a lament psalm—as a model, Alex composed his own prayer of lament in which he honestly voiced his struggles. On the one hand, his growing grasp of God's goodness and grace kept him from accusing God of wrongdoing. On the other hand he could raise the hard questions typical of biblical lamentations: "Where were you, God, when this happened? And how did you feel? Could you show me how you responded?"

These questions propelled the counseling agenda for several sessions. Alex began to see that the Lord had been on site in his life all along. Although he was not a Christian when victimized, the truth of God's electing grace assured Alex that even then he was in God's mind. His counselor helped Alex to see God's righteous anger against the perpetrators and God's promise to judge such evil (Rom. 12:19). Studying the compassion of God helped Alex see how God compassionately wept for the abuse he had suffered. God had good purposes in permitting such a horrible trial.

What gracious purposes did Alex identify? He saw that God's agenda was to lead him, as a boy then and a man now, to call on Christ and seek his help. God intended this tragedy to teach Alex to trust in God and not in himself.

Furthermore, God was using this painful experience to cultivate greater compassion for fellow-sufferers (in whatever form of suffering), and to equip Alex for wiser, gentler, and more fruitful ministry to others. Today he is a merciful minister of Jesus to others.

Conclusion

What should you do when you are tempted to blame God for your suffering? How should you counsel those who are angry at him? How can you steer a middle course between stoic denial and fleshly venting?

First, reaffirm your belief in God's sovereignty, power, wisdom, and goodness toward you in Christ. Begin by meditating on the passages listed above and talking to God in prayer about what his Word is teaching you. Supplement your Scripture reading with biblically sound books on learning to trust God amidst suffering.[5]

Second, reject the blasphemous temptation to accuse God of evil or cast aspersions on his character or purposes. Spurn the "it's okay to be angry at God" therapeutic voices of our day.

Third, recognize your limited ability to fathom God's decrees. Your finite, fallen mind is simply incapable of comprehending his ways. You are not responsible for figuring out God; only for knowing, trusting, and pleasing him. Resist the demand to know God's secret things, and instead rest in God's revealed things (Deut. 29:29), what his Word tells you about his loving purposes. Confess to him your ignorance of his hidden ways and affirm your essential, albeit weak or confused, faith in his goodness. Remember the cross as the final proof that God loves you (Rom. 5:8) and he is for you amid your sufferings (Rom. 8:28–39).

Fourth, learn to acknowledge to God, in honest faith and submission, your thoughts and feelings. Be transparent in his presence; "pour out your hearts to him" (Ps. 62:8). Express your thoughts and feelings, your doubts and questions, your joys and sorrows, your groans and sighs. Yet do so with reverence. Confess to the Lord any anger you might be holding against him. Don't vent it; repent of it!

Fifth, as you learn to bring your thoughts and feelings in line with God's good purposes, be careful to obey him. Do what God commands even when it differs from your desires.

Notice Carolyn's renewed perspective: "Heavenly Father, I hate what Ray has done. It hurts. And there are times when, for the life of me, I don't know why you let this happen to the kids and me. I know you are in control but it's hard to see your hand in all this mess, and I am tempted to get angry with you. Help me, Lord. I know deep down that you are good, that you love me and are using this to make me like Jesus. Help me to trust you and not doubt you. And help me to do what pleases you in this situation, even when I'm upset."

When tempted to be angry at God, we need not settle for cold stoicism or hot blasphemy. God opens the door for us to lament, to bring him our doubts and questions—wisely, humbly, and honestly. He inclines his ear to his suffering people. May the Lord spur us to renewed faith, holiness, and humility as we walk with him.

Notes

1 Kay Arthur, "But I'm So Angry!" in *Lord, Heal My Hurts* (Sisters, Oregon: Multnomah, 1989).

2 John Calvin, *Sermons from Job*. Selected and translated by Leroy Nixon (Grand Rapids: Eerdmans, 1952), 29–30.

3 Ibid.

4 Ibid.

5 I recommend Jerry Bridges, *Trusting God: Even When Life Hurts* (Colorado Springs: NavPress, 1988); his booklet, *You Can Trust God* (Colorado Springs: NavPress, 1989); Joni Eareckson Tada and Steven Estes, *When God Weeps: Why Our Sufferings Matter to the Almighty* (Grand Rapids: Zondervan, 1997); and John J. Murray's booklet, *Behind a Frowning Providence* (Carlisle, Pa.: Banner of Truth, 1990).

***Robert D. Jones** is pastor of Grace Fellowship Church in Hurricane, West Virginia.*

RCL Ministry Booklets

A.D.D.: Wandering Minds and Wired Bodies, by Edward T. Welch

Anger: Escaping the Maze, by David Powlison

Angry at God?: Bring Him Your Doubts and Questions, by Robert D. Jones

Depression: The Way Up When You Are Down, by Edward T. Welch

Domestic Abuse: How to Help, by David Powlison, Paul David Tripp, and Edward T. Welch

Forgiveness: "I Just Can't Forgive Myself!" by Robert D. Jones

God's Love: Better than Unconditional, by David Powlison

Homosexuality: Speaking the Truth in Love, by Edward T. Welch

"Just One More": When Desires Don't Take No for an Answer, by Edward T. Welch

Marriage: Whose Dream? by Paul David Tripp

Motives: "Why Do I Do the Things I Do?" by Edward T. Welch

Pornography: Slaying the Dragon, by David Powlison

Pre-Engagement: 5 Questions to Ask Yourselves, by David Powlison and John Yenchko

Priorities: Mastering Time Management, by James C. Petty

Sexual Sin: Combatting the Drifting and Cheating, by Jeffrey S. Black

Suffering: Eternity Makes a Difference, by Paul David Tripp

Teens and Sex: How Should We Teach Them? by Paul David Tripp

Thankfulness: Even When It Hurts, by Susan Lutz